Fostering Creativity

Pocket Mentor Series

The Pocket Mentor Series offers immediate solutions to common challenges managers face on the job every day. Each book in the series is packed with handy tools, self-tests, and real-life examples to help you identify your strengths and weaknesses and hone critical skills. Whether you're at your desk, in a meeting, or on the road, these portable guides enable you to tackle the daily demands of your work with greater speed, savvy, and effectiveness.

Books in the series

Fostering Creativity

Creativity
Expert Solutions to Everyday Challenges

Harvard Business Press

Boston, Massachusetts

Significant portions of this work, including core concepts, are derived from the
book *When Sparks Fly: Igniting Creativity in Groups* by Dorothy Leonard and
Walter Swap (Harvard Business School Press, 1999).

Library of Congress Cataloging-in-Publication Data

Fostering creativity : expert solutions to everyday challenges.
    p. cm. — (Pocket mentor series)
  Includes bibliographical references.
  ISBN 978-1-4221-2893-0 (pbk. : alk. paper)   1. Creative ability in business.
2. Creative thinking.   3. Problem solving. I. Harvard Business School.
  HD53.F676 2010
  658.3'14—dc22

                                                              2009038802

The paper used in this publication meets the requirements of the American National
Standard for Permanence of Paper for Publications and Documents in Libraries
and Archives Z39.48-1992.

Contents

Fostering Creativity: The Basics

Tips and Tools

Mentor's Message: Why Fostering Creativity Is Important

Is your group having trouble generating new business ideas? Is the group thinking too much along traditional lines, or having difficulty thinking very far down the road? Is your group reluctant to take risks? If so, your organization may be missing out on the creativity it needs to solve key business problems and generate valuable innovations. And in today's hypercompetitive environment, an organization that cannot innovate cannot expect to survive for long.

Is there anything you can do as a manager to unleash your group's creativity? Yes. Essentially, all the situations described above stem from a problem in the creative functioning of the group. Contrary to what many people believe, group creativity doesn't just happen—it can be planned for, nurtured, and enhanced.

And you can help. The way you manage the various personalities in your team can help unleash your team's creative potential. But this is demanding work. You start by developing a deep appreciation for the different thinking styles in your team. Then you consciously try to have those differing approaches rub up against one another—making sure that the resulting "abrasion" improves rather than undermines the quality of the group's work.

There are other steps you can take as well. By paying close attention to group norms, you can foster a climate in which people feel good about their work and are motivated to seek out problems and solve them. You can alter the physical workspace in ways that make for more robust, stimulating communication. And you can lead your group through structured thinking exercises that will help them make connections they might not have made otherwise.

Using content derived from the book *When Sparks Fly* by Dorothy Leonard and Walter Swap, this book explains how to make all these innovations happen—so that your organization can benefit from the fresh ideas flowing from your team.

Dorothy Leonard, Mentor

Dorothy Leonard is the William J. Abernathy Professor Emerita of Business Administration at Harvard Business School, where she has taught courses in corporate creativity, new product and process design, knowledge management, and innovation.

Professor Leonard is the author of two books on innovation, *Wellsprings of Knowledge: Building and Sustaining the Sources of Innovation* and *When Sparks Fly: Igniting Group Creativity*. Professor Leonard's major research interests, consulting expertise, and teaching efforts relate to creativity and managing the innovation process.

Fostering Creativity: The Basics

What Is Creativity?

The word *creativity* crops up in many workplace conversations. But what does it mean, exactly? Is it the same as innovation? Can anyone be creative? Is there a distinct process through which creativity unfolds? In the pages that follow, we explore these and other questions regarding the nature of creativity.

A definition

You know creativity when you see it, right? Not necessarily. But a deeper understanding of what creativity is—and what it is not—can help you enhance the creativity of any group you lead. Let's start with a definition. In its simplest terms, creativity is a process of developing and expressing novel ideas that are likely to be useful.

CREATIVITY: a process of developing and expressing novel ideas that are likely to be useful.

This definition raises two points that are important to understand regarding creativity:

Creativity is not so much a talent as it is a goal-oriented process. Making your group more creative is not a matter of importing a few people who have creative character traits and then relying on these folks to generate all your breakthrough ideas. Rather, it's a matter of designing a collaborative approach that maximizes everyone's distinctive gifts, experience, and expertise. Moreover, the purpose or goal of the creative process is to solve a particular problem or satisfy a specific need.

Creativity involves convergent as well as divergent thinking. The creative process begins with *divergent thinking*—a breaking away from familiar or established ways of seeing and doing that produces novel ideas. *Convergent thinking* occurs in the later stages of the process. As the original ideas generated by the divergent thinking are communicated to others, they are evaluated to determine which of them are genuinely novel and worth pursuing. The group then uses convergent thinking to choose an option with the potential to solve the problem that initiated the creative process. You'll learn more about divergent and convergent thinking later in this book.

How creativity relates to innovation

You've seen the definition for creativity. Now let's consider how creativity relates to innovation. Again, we need a definition. Simply put, innovation is the embodiment, combination, and/or synthesis of knowledge in original, relevant, valued new products, processes, or services.

INNOVATION: the embodiment, combination, and/or synthesis of knowledge in original, relevant, valued new products, processes, or services.

An innovation is *the end result of the creative process*. Again, creativity is a process you employ to improve your problem solving.

So you're not done until your creative efforts have produced a product, service, or process that answers the original need or solves the problem you identified at the outset.

Five misconceptions about creativity

Quite a bit of research on creativity has been done over the years. In the course of all this experimentation and exploration, it's become clear that creativity is a widely misunderstood subject. Misconceptions about this seemingly mysterious process abound. Below, we examine five of them. After reading them, ask yourself whether *you* hold any of these misconceptions about creativity. If so, doing away with them will help you extend your managerial arena—the range of possible actions you can take to maximize your group's creative potential.

Misconception #1: **The smarter you are, the more creative you are.** Intelligence correlates with creativity only up to a point. Once you have enough intelligence to do your job, the relationship no longer holds. That is, above a fairly modest threshold—an IQ of about 120—there is no correlation between intelligence and creativity.

Misconception #2: **The young are more creative than the old.** Age is not a clear predictor of creative potential. Research shows that it usually takes seven to ten years to build up deep expertise in a given field—the kind of expertise that enables a person to perceive patterns of order or meaning that are invisible to the novice. Thus, in the business world, the necessary creativity can be found in an adult of any age. At the same time, however, expertise can *inhibit* creativity: experts sometimes find it difficult to see or think outside established patterns.

Misconception #3: **Creativity is reserved for the few—the flamboyant high rollers.** The willingness to take calculated risks and the ability to think in unconventional ways *do* play a role in creativity. But that doesn't mean that creativity is restricted to high-impact, high-risk endeavors. You don't have to be a bungee jumper in order to be creative. In fact, you don't have to be markedly different from everyone else. Moreover, managers can take specific steps to help themselves and anyone else be more creative. On rare occasions, the ideas that a creative person comes up with will be visionary leaps forward that revolutionize an industry. But more often, they will be small improvements that advance the organizational cause.

Misconception #4: **The creative act is essentially solitary.** In fact, a high percentage of the world's most important inventions resulted not from the work of one lone genius, but from the collaboration of a group of people with complementary skills. Individuals and groups that make important discoveries pass through a number of stages. The stage of illumination, when a flash of insight occurs, is the next-to-last stage. Although this stage tends to attract all the press, most innovations come about only after much toil, many dead ends, and more than a few apparent breakthroughs that ultimately don't pan out.

Misconception #5: **You can't manage creativity.** Granted, creativity is rather like a genie that can't be bottled: you can never know in advance who will be involved in a creative act, what that act will be, or precisely when or how it will occur. Nevertheless, as a manager, you can create the conditions that make creativity much more likely to occur. That is, you can increase the probability of innovation.

So what's the lesson behind these five misconceptions? Your group has the potential to be creative—and thus to be innovative. But to unleash that potential, you need to set up the proper conditions. As we'll see in the next sections of the book, setting up those conditions calls for a specific series of actions. You'll need to:

- Carefully determine the composition of your group.

- Enrich the workplace environment—the psychological and the physical environment.

- Provide tools and techniques that enhance idea generation.

- Manage the creative process so that the best insights and ideas are translated into innovative products, services, and ways of doing business.

A good place to start is to become familiar with the sequence of the creative process.

The creative process

Think of the creative process as consisting of the following four steps:

1. **Assemble your team:** You select group members specifically to maximize creativity.

2. **Identify opportunities:** Group members identify a problem requiring creativity and (ultimately) innovation.

3. **Generate options:** Through divergent thinking, group members come up with an array of options for seizing the opportunity they've identified.

4. **Converge on the one best option:** Group members come to agreement on which of the options at hand will best solve the problem they've identified and create the most valuable new product, service, or way of doing business.

The creative process is not as linear as the above list of stages might suggest, but each phase is vital to group creativity. As a manager, you'll need to ensure that your group progresses through each stage.

In the sections that follow, we'll look at each of these steps in closer detail.

Step 1: Assemble Your Team

Creativity thrives when the right mix of people come together to work on a problem or exploit an opportunity. Not just any blend will do. To assemble a creative team, you need to understand why such a team is valuable, what characteristics distinguish it from other teams, why intellectual diversity is an essential element of the team, and how to source and integrate team members. We discuss each of these matters below.

The value of creative teams

Creative work is fueled by a blend of talents and personal attributes that rarely exist in one person. For example, the work requires an ability to see problems through fresh eyes, as well as a flair for planning how to turn a creative idea into a profitable innovation.

For this reason, creative teams—groups in which different members contribute different, complementary skills—are increasingly important in today's economy. A creative team ensures a level of output that is greater than each individual could achieve working alone.

Of course, as the manager, you're also a member of the team—and you can take steps to enhance your own creative potential as well. See "Steps for enhancing your creative potential" for ideas.

Steps for enhancing your creative potential

1. **Strive for alignment.** Make sure that the goals of the organization you work for are consonant with your most cherished values. Instead of considering jobs at which you excel, think instead about jobs that match your deeply embedded life interests.

2. **Pursue some self-initiated activity.** Choose projects that inherently interest and motivate you. If you have always loved graphic design, try to determine why the packaging for one of your company's products leaves customers cold.

3. **Be open to serendipity.** Develop a bias toward action and toward trying new ideas. For instance, if an accident or failure occurs while you're prototyping a new LCD screen, don't dismiss it too quickly. Study it for the learning opportunity that may lie within. Each day, write down what surprised you and how you surprised others.

4. **Diversify your stimuli.** Intellectual cross-pollination promotes thinking in new directions. Develop cross-functional skills: rotate into every job you are capable of doing. Get to know people who spark your imagination. Become a lifelong learner: take classes unrelated to your work. Bring your insights from outside interests or activities to bear on your workplace challenges.

5. **Create opportunities for informal communication.** Take advantage of unexpected opportunities to exchange ideas with colleagues. Creative thought often happens during spontaneous

interactions between individuals. Such interactions, however, are useful only if real communication occurs. You must find ways to encourage and facilitate communication that is appropriate for the creative environment.

Characteristics of creative teams

To build a team that produces maximum creative output, you must carefully examine the group's composition. You need to make sure that your group as a whole has all the requisite skills and attributes needed to generate creative ideas.

A good place to start is by considering the paradoxical characteristics that distinguish a creative team from other teams. Table 1 shows tendencies of thought and action that appear to be mutually exclusive or contradictory but somehow manage to exist side by side in a creative team.

TABLE 1

A paradoxical blend

A creative team must demonstrate . . .	While also demonstrating . . .
Beginner's mind	Experience
Freedom	Discipline
Play	Professionalism
Improvisation	Planning

For example, to do its best work, your group needs deep knowledge of the subjects relevant to the problem it's trying to solve, as well as a mastery of the processes involved. But at the same time, your group needs fresh perspectives that are unencumbered by the prevailing wisdom or established ways of operating. Often called a "beginner's mind," this is the perspective of a newcomer: someone who is curious, even playful, and willing to ask anything—because he doesn't know what he doesn't know.

Spotlight on intellectual diversity

In addition to demonstrating the paradoxical blend of qualities described above, a team must exhibit *intellectual diversity* if it hopes to be creative. Intellectual diversity is present when team members bring to the table different areas of expertise and deep knowledge of a range of disciplines, as well as a variety of preferred thinking styles.

What is a preferred thinking style? It's the unconscious way a person looks at and interacts with the world. When faced with a problem or dilemma, a person will usually approach it by thinking in the way in which she is most comfortable. And although each style has particular advantages, no one style is better than another.

An intellectually diverse group thinks creatively and is likely to generate innovative products, services, and ways of doing business based on the fresh ideas it develops. You can't *make* people adopt a thinking style other than the one they prefer, but you *can* mix thinking styles in such a way that the ideas and solutions generated by your group are all the richer and more valuable for the variety of perspectives that inform them.

Note: Intellectual diversity is not the same as ethnic and gender diversity, which often enhance a group's range of thought but don't guarantee it. Just as people of the same gender or ethnic group don't necessarily think alike, you can't assume that people from different groups think differently. So even as you consider the ethnic and gender representation of your group, focus on preferred thinking styles, functional specialties, and the particular skills that influence how a person approaches a problem.

> *It requires a very unusual mind to undertake the obvious.*
> —Alfred North Whitehead

There are many different ways to describe how people think and make decisions. For the purposes of ensuring that your group has all the characteristics necessary for creative work, what's most important is that you develop the ability to recognize and describe different thinking styles.

The Myers-Briggs Type Indicator breaks down thinking preferences into four categories, with two opposite tendencies in each category. Table 2 provides more details.

Don't get hung up on the actual word used to describe a particular thinking tendency represented in the Myers-Briggs model. Everyone exhibits all eight of these tendencies, but they do so in varying degrees. For example, a feeling person is not incapable of logical thought. Rather, his or her thinking about a decision tends to be guided by the decision's emotional impact on key relationships.

Start with yourself: how would you characterize your own thinking style? Knowing your own preferences helps you appreciate other

TABLE 2

Opposing Myers-Briggs Type Indicators

Extroverted: These people look to other people as the primary means of processing information.

Introverted: These people tend to process information internally first before presenting the results to others.

Sensing: These people tend to prefer hard data, concrete facts—information that is closely tied to the five senses.

Intuitive: These people are more comfortable with ideas and concepts, with the "big picture."

Thinking: These people prefer logical processes and orderly ways of approaching problems.

Feeling: These people are more attuned to emotional cues; they are more likely to make decisions based on the values or relationships involved.

Judging: These people tend to prefer closure—they like having all the loose ends tied up.

Perceiving: These people like things more open; they tend to be more comfortable with ambiguity and often want to collect still more data before reaching a decision.

thinking styles—you begin to understand how different perspectives can complement or round out your own. You may be particularly good at generating unusual ideas. But for those ideas to lead to something productive, your team will also need people with strong analytical skills who can assess whether your novel ideas fit the criteria your customers require. In addition, your team will need people with the practical intelligence necessary to translate your idea into a product or service.

Hiring for creativity

Once you've assessed how the thinking styles of your team members complement (or duplicate) your own, you'll have a pretty good sense of whether any gaps exist. If the team lacks vital skills or expertise, you're going to have to look outside your group to find what you need.

> *When all men think alike, no one thinks very much.*
> —Walter Lippmann

First, look elsewhere within your organization. Are there people with different thinking styles or skills who could temporarily take part in the work of your team? If not, you'll need to go outside your organization—maybe even outside your industry.

For instance, when engineers working at a ceramics manufacturer were having difficulty getting the ceramics to release from their molds, they realized that their problem had to do with quick-freezing, not with ceramics. So instead of seeking out other ceramics experts, they turned to the experts in quick-freezing: the food industry.

On those occasions when you are able to hire new employees, take full advantage of the opportunity to hire for creativity. Look for:

- People whose intellectual perspectives complement (rather than duplicate) your own preferred styles and skills and those of others in your group.

- A balance between professional expertise and desirable personal characteristics (such as initiative, ability to get along with others, etc.) in each new hire.

- People who are able and willing to work across functional boundaries.

When you define hiring criteria, put a premium on increasing your group's intellectual diversity and finding necessary skills that the group currently lacks. Don't simply list a standard set of skills.

Also consider exploring nontraditional hiring channels (beyond your company's human resources department). For example, consider interns who've spent a summer or semester with your company. Ask colleagues for referrals. Tell friends outside your industry to be on the lookout for people whose skill sets match your needs.

Remember: if your goal is to build a truly creative group, it won't be enough just to hire *one* person who has a different perspective. A lone hire soon feels isolated and becomes marginalized. For the diverse thinking styles to *make a difference,* you need to hire a critical mass of newcomers with fresh perspectives.

Integrating team members

Your work doesn't stop after you hire new team members or bring in several from elsewhere in your organization. It's now up to you to take the initiative to ensure that new members are thoroughly integrated into the functioning of the team. The following tactics can help:

- Discuss with group members why it is valuable to have people with different perspectives and skills.

- Match newcomers up with mentors—other team members who can help them acclimate quickly.

- Make sure that group members who represent different skills and perspectives will be able to demonstrate their value to the group—even if it's only in small ways at the outset.

- Meet regularly with new members to discuss their experience with the group and to address any difficulties.

- Make certain that a new member's role within the group is clear to everyone.

- Include all team members in social events.

It takes time and careful thought to assemble a creative team. But the investment will pay big dividends. You'll end up with a group that can not only generate fresh ideas but also translate those ideas into new forms of value for customers and your overall organization.

Step 2: Identify Opportunities

Once you've assembled your creative team, it's time to identify opportunities to capitalize on through fresh thinking. You can find opportunities inside your organization as well as outside.

Finding opportunities inside your organization

Most successful innovation results from a conscious, purposeful search for opportunities to exploit through fresh, creative thinking. Some areas of opportunity inside a company represent more fertile ground than others, for example:

- **Unexpected occurrences.** The loss of an overseas factory due to political upheaval presents an opportunity to find other ways to manufacture your organization's offerings.

- **Incongruities.** Acquisition of another firm by your company creates the opportunity to define a new corporate strategy.

- **Process needs.** To illustrate, your division will be introducing a new product line—which presents the opportunity to create separate distribution channels.

The world is but a canvas to the imagination.
—Henry David Thoreau

Finding opportunities outside your organization

Don't make the all-too-common mistake of focusing only on creative opportunities inside your organization. Changes in the outside world present a rich array of possibilities as well, for example:

- **Demographic shifts.** As the population ages, demand for leisure activities and convenience products grows—presenting opportunities to develop new products and services to satisfy that demand.

- **Perceptual changes.** Market surveys reveal that consumers are losing awareness of your company's brand—the set of qualities that distinguish it from competitors. This trend presents an opportunity to find ways to strengthen your company's brand equity.

- **New knowledge and technology.** To illustrate, a new manufacturing technology presents opportunities for your company to reduce its production costs significantly.

Looking for an area in which to concentrate your creative efforts? Use these categories to help you make that assessment. Another approach is to list all the aspects of your company's operations that require special knowledge or expertise and to concentrate your efforts there.

Finally, you can further help your group identify opportunities by providing members with outside stimulation—exposing them to events and individuals who can get them thinking about changes

What Would YOU Do?

Got Intellectual Diversity?

JOSÉ WAS IN CHARGE of launching an aggressive marketing plan for a new line of mountaineering equipment at GetOut, Inc. He saw himself as an analytical thinker, and over the years he had built a team of marketing professionals who had a thinking style similar to his. Before the project got under way, his friend Marta in HR suggested that he bring in people with different skill sets to enhance the "intellectual diversity" of his group.

José found the idea intriguing but was worried that different skill sets would translate into different ways of thinking, different expectations, and very different personalities. All that diversity could mean chaos, and that made José nervous. "How will we get anything done," he asked himself, "if we're disagreeing all the time?"

What would YOU do? The mentor will suggest a solution in *What You COULD Do.*

---

going on in the business arena and the possibilities these changes might present. "Tips for providing outside stimulation for your group" offers ideas.

Tips for providing outside stimulation for your group

- Bring in paid or unpaid interns: students, people making job transitions, and so on.
- Bring in day visitors to participate in brainstorming sessions or other activities with the group.
- Bring in temporary group members, such as people on sabbatical from universities or other organizations.
- Arrange reciprocal visits with other groups or organizations.
- Bring in a speaker to present a unique perspective or expertise. (Remember to look outside your industry or specialty.)
- Arrange a site visit to a customer, a customer of one of your customers, or even a competitor.
- Arrange a field trip outside your industry to observe best practices—for example, an airline hoping to improve customer service might visit a clothing retailer known for its excellent standards in this area.
- Meet with independent inventors or entrepreneurs in your field.
- Surf the Web to explore competitors' sites.
- Surf the Web to find out how people in other industries are using the Web to fulfill the same functions that you perform.
- Bring in consultants to provide different perspectives.
- Arrange workshops or training in needed skills or processes.

What You COULD Do.

Remember José's nervousness about creating more intellectual diversity in his team?

Here's what the mentor suggests:

Chaos at the beginning of the creative process is a good thing. In order to generate fresh, new ideas that push the boundaries, José should invite people with varying points of view and divergent areas of expertise to join his team. For example, he could include someone from Sales who would represent the voice of the customer, and someone from Product Development who's good at generating unusual ideas. When people with different thinking styles and expertise interact, they may indeed have conflicting points of view. But they will also likely generate more creative ideas that will in turn yield a more original, creative marketing campaign.

Step 3:
Generate Options

Once you and your group have identified an opportunity that could be exploited through creative thinking, it's time to generate options for capitalizing on that opportunity. Here's where you'll need to manage the dynamics in your group carefully. You want all those thinking styles to rub up against one another—producing "creative abrasion." But you don't want the resulting clash of opinions and ideas to turn destructive.

Below are some ideas for managing creative abrasion, encouraging the divergent thinking that leads to creativity, using structured brainstorming techniques to generate options, and establishing a psychological and physical environment conducive to creativity.

Managing creative abrasion

When several different thinking styles clash, creative sparks fly. That's the insight behind the phrase *creative abrasion*. Make no mistake about it: intellectual diversity does have its hazards. When you put people with divergent ways of thinking together on one team, the result will not be unbroken harmony—nor would you want it to be. Expect to have disagreements and clashes—that way, you won't be surprised when they occur. But you must be vigilant nonetheless, constantly asking yourself if the conflict is creative or not.

For creative abrasion to work, you have to maintain a dynamic equilibrium. You want to foster the kind of abrasion that gets team members interacting, listening to one another's points of view, and questioning one another's assumptions. But you don't want the conflict to become personal, or the group will splinter and productivity will suffer. (See "Steps for depersonalizing conflict.")

One way to manage creative abrasion is to establish group norms, or rules, for interacting. By reminding team members of the agreed-upon ways of behaving, you help restore a sense of team identity and turn conflict into something substantive and productive.

What should your group's operating guidelines be? That depends on the purpose of the group and the personalities of its members. Certainly, however, any effective set of norms should be clear and concise, and should also include these basic rules:

- Respect all members of the group.

- Commit to active listening.

- Agree on how to voice concerns and handle conflict.

To guarantee the free flow of ideas, some groups may want to go further—for example, explicitly stating that anyone is entitled to disagree with anyone else. They may also want to adopt specific guidelines that

- Support calculated risk taking

- Establish procedures about acknowledging and handling failure

- Foster individual expression

- Encourage a playful attitude

Whatever principles and norms your group defines, make sure all the members participate in establishing them—and are willing to abide by them.

Steps for depersonalizing conflict

1. **Grant legitimacy to others and give them the benefit of the doubt. Assume that:**
   - Others are trying to do the right thing
   - Others may see things that you miss
   - You may see things that others miss
   - Conflicting views are an important source of learning
2. **Allow all parties to the conflict a chance to speak.** Without interruption, have all parties to the conflict:
   - Describe the data on which they based their decisions (observations, reading, reports, etc.)
   - Use their own words to describe what they saw or heard
   - Give reasons for their interpretations
   - Explain why they decided on the action they took (or want to take)
3. **Seek to understand the differences between individuals.** For example, ask others to comment on the interpretation of data and then identify alternative interpretations.
4. **Reconcile the various actions/decisions desired by taking into account all the data and interpretations uncovered.**

Encouraging divergent thinking

Creative ideas arise from the application of *divergent thinking*—through which team members:

- See connections among facts or events that others have missed

- Ask questions that haven't been asked before

- Ask questions from different perspectives

The goal of divergent thinking is to quickly generate a wide variety of options for exploiting an opportunity the team has identified—without yet judging the merits of those options. Brainstorming can be a powerful tool for divergent thinking in your team.

Using brainstorming techniques

Brainstorming builds a team's *fluency* (its ability to produce many original ideas easily) and its *flexibility* (the ability to come up with many different kinds of ideas). But for a brainstorming exercise to succeed, your team must apply four key principles:

1. Focus the brainstorming on an actual problem that your group is trying to solve. In other words, your brainstorming should be bound by real-world constraints.

2. Suspend judgment while ideas are being generated. Even the wildest ideas are to be encouraged, because the quantity of ideas affects the quality of the final decision.

3. Limit the discussion to one conversation at a time, and keep it focused on the topic.

4. Encourage team members to build on one another's ideas.

> *Creativity involves breaking out of established patterns*
> *in order to look at things in a different way.*
> —Edward de Bono

Brainstorming techniques fall into four broad categories: visioning, exploring, modifying, and experimenting. Each category uses a different thought process, but there are some commonalities as well. For example, visioning and exploring techniques both start with the intuitive process and end with information gathering and data analysis. By contrast, modifying and experimenting techniques start with existing data and use intuition to draw ideas from those facts.

Brainstorming technique #1: Visioning. This approach asks group members to imagine in detail both a long-term, ideal solution and the means of achieving it. The idea is to break free of the ingrained practicality that inhibits innovative thought. Have your team begin by ignoring constraints. Ask, "If money, time, and resources were no object, what ideas would produce the ideal future?" For example, "If our consulting company could provide *any* services, which services would you choose?"

As you and your team try to imagine the ideal future, follow what intrigues you—a breakthrough idea often comes from a seemingly irrelevant source. Use the following three strategies to help people on your team imagine an ideal future:

1. **Wish List**: Ask your team members to "let themselves go" and imagine an ideal situation in which they would be granted any wish they wanted. Encourage everyone to review their lists: what did they discover about themselves or the situation?

2. **The Ideal Scenario**: Ask the group to imagine what the ideal solution would look like. This can be done with words or images. For example, team members could pore over magazines, select images, and paste them together in a collage. Follow the creation with discussion and exploration.

3. **Time Machine**: Ask team members to pretend that they can travel five to seven years into the future. What would the situation look like then? What would the team have accomplished? Add whatever questions are relevant to the creative challenge being explored.

Once you've generated several ideas that would constitute an ideal future, ask what it would take to make those ideas happen. How would you actually bring about the ideas you've envisioned?

Brainstorming technique #2: Exploring. Use guided imagery—symbols, analogies, and metaphors—to explore potentially fruitful options. For instance, if your group is trying to create a new, truly innovative customer service, you could ask, "If customer service were music, what music comes to mind when you think of best-practice service?" Or, "What are the feelings that you want your ideal level of service to generate in customers—and what are the sensory images that come to mind when you envision that service?"

A variation of the exploring method is to take your working assumptions and literally reverse them. The new possibilities that emerge are often fruitful. For example, suppose your team has been assuming that it will receive funding for the project resulting from its creative process. Challenge the team to generate ideas for how it would exploit the opportunity in question if it *didn't* receive any funding.

Brainstorming technique #3: Modifying. Whereas visioning techniques begin by assuming that there are no constraints, modifying techniques begin with the status quo—with current technology or conditions—and seek to make adaptations.

For instance, let's say you and your team work at a software company that makes applications used by graphic designers. One effective way to discover how to modify or adapt your current product or service is to try to look at the offering as though you were a customer. For example, ask team members to imagine themselves as designers who want a new program. What features or functionality would they like the program to include?

Brainstorming technique #4: Experimenting. Experimenting entails systematically combining elements of your team's thinking in various ways and then testing the combinations. One experimental approach involves creating a matrix. For example, a car wash owner in search of a new market or market extension would begin by listing parameters across the top of the matrix: method, products washed, equipment, and products sold. Under each parameter, he would list all the possible variations he can think of. For instance, the equipment variations might include sprays, conveyors, stalls, dryers, and brushes. The products washed might include cars, houses, clothes, and dogs. The resulting table allows him to put together new business possibilities using alternatives listed in each column. Thus, he might decide to start a service for pet owners to wash their dogs using his existing stalls and brushes.

"Tips for facilitating brainstorming sessions" presents some additional recommendations for using all four brainstorming techniques described above.

Tips for facilitating brainstorming sessions

- You may want to include some customers, noncustomers, or competitors' customers in the brainstorming session.
- Be sure to provide any supporting infrastructure needed—flip charts, a table covered in paper to be used for doodling and note taking, or even an electronic whiteboard.
- In coming up with possible solutions or ideas, be as concrete as possible. You may want to draw or represent some of the ideas visually.
- Don't assume that it's business as usual, that this problem or challenge is similar to ones that have come before.
- Set high aspirations—stretch goals for what you'd like your group to achieve.

- Don't fall in love with the first possible option your team comes up with; generate as many ideas as you can before evaluating and prioritizing them.
- Remember that productive brainstorming sessions are the result of skillful facilitation.

Creating the right psychological environment

Group norms are important for establishing a psychological climate that promotes creativity, but they will get you only so far. If you want team members to believe that the norms are for real, you have to back them up with your own actions and with your organization's reward system.

Your actions. What you say you value most highly and how you actually respond to events and individuals in your team often turn out to be two very different things. For example, perhaps your group has established the norm that "everyone will have a say without being interrupted"—but you find yourself interrupting some group members. Any dissonance between the agreed-upon norms and your own behavior as a manager can spawn distrust in your group—which will only hamper its creativity.

To make sure there is no such dissonance, ask team members to fill out anonymous evaluation forms from time to time, in which they assess whether your behavior fosters the agreed-upon norms, such as free-flowing communication or a willingness to take risks.

You can also act in ways that help team members feel safe while talking about concerns they might have about how the team is functioning. For example, some people may have been frustrated by another team member who hasn't been contributing ideas. A difficult, unspoken issue can be thought of as a "moose on the table"—a large problem that everyone knows is there but no one feels safe discussing. See "Steps for making it safe to discuss a 'moose'" for guidelines on how to facilitate such discussions while your team is generating options.

Steps for making it safe to discuss a "moose"

1. **Create a climate in which people are willing to discuss difficult issues.** As the manager, you need to help your team understand the concept of "a moose on the table" (a significant issue or problem that is impeding progress because everyone is ignoring it). You also need to initiate a conversation about how the team should handle such unspoken issues—before a specific situation arises. Use this checklist to set the stage.
   - Introduce the concept of a "moose on the table" when you are establishing your team principles.
   - Legitimize the process of identifying a moose. Make it clear that you *want* problems to be pointed out—that even though the subject may seem taboo, no one will be penalized for pointing out a moose.
   - Also, make sure that all team members understand that *anyone* can point out a moose: the right to raise an issue should not be confined to "higher" ranks alone.
   - Encourage the use of humor—it helps prevent people from being defensive. For instance, buy a big, stuffed-toy moose

and make it available for team members to pick up and place in the center of the table when the time comes to discuss a sensitive concern.

2. **Facilitate the discussion.** How do you manage a moose once it has been identified? Use the following guidelines:

- If someone points out a moose, it is important to stop whatever you are doing, at least briefly, to acknowledge the issue. Even if you disagree that a problem exists, you must concede that, to one person at least, it does. Otherwise, team members will not feel inclined to bring up such issues in the future.

- Refer back to your team principles. As a manager, it is your job to remind the team how you have all agreed to treat one another.

- Encourage the person who identified the moose to be specific and to use examples.

- Keep the discussion impersonal. The point is not to assign blame—discuss *what* is impeding progress, not *who*.

- If the issue involves someone's behavior, encourage the person who identified the problem to explain how the behavior affects him or her, rather than making assumptions about the motivation behind the behavior. For example, if someone is not contributing ideas during brainstorming sessions, you might say, "When you don't contribute, the team can't be sure we've accumulated a full range of options," not, "You don't seem to be excited about this project."

- Discuss why the topic is taboo.

3. Move toward closure by discussing what can be done.
   - Try to leave with some concrete suggestions for alleviating the problem, if not a complete solution.
   - If the subject is too sensitive and discussions are going nowhere, consider adjourning the meeting until a (specified) later date so that people can cool down. Or consider bringing in a facilitator to help keep discussions on an impersonal level.

Your organization's reward system. You can further help your team generate options by ensuring that your company's reward system—particularly incentives and means of recognition—supports rather than suppresses creativity.

Creativity will not flourish without a reward system that encourages individuals to stretch their ideas, try totally new approaches, and push beyond the bounds of normal work processes. Creative energy is a limited resource and must be replenished not just at the end of the creative process, but throughout the project's life cycle. An exhausted or discouraged group cannot maintain its creativity. Rewards serve to rejuvenate and refresh creative energy.

There are many ways to help people feel motivated and energized to work creatively. Rewards can be based on a number of mechanisms:

- **Recognition**—for example, acknowledging an individual or group with a plaque or public announcement

- **Control**—allowing an individual or group to participate in making a decision or choice that affects them, or giving a group the resources it needs to carry out a project

- **Celebration**—for example, acknowledging a successful new-product launch by throwing a party

- **Rejuvenation**—providing time off or away from the task

Another way to think about rewards is in terms of *how* they motivate. A reward can either be

- **Intrinsic**—something that appeals to a person's desire for self-actualization or challenge, to her deep interest and involvement in the work, or to her curiosity or sense of enjoyment

- **Extrinsic**—something that appeals to a person's desire to attain a goal that is distinct from the work itself. Examples can include incentive pay, a luxury vacation given as a reward for generating the most profitable new idea, or special recognition for meeting an important deadline

When work is not routine—which is the case with creative work—you need to rely on the power of intrinsic motivation to generate creative thought. In other words, you must make sure that any rewards or incentives you establish don't become more important than the work itself, thereby undermining team members' intrinsic motivation.

At the same time, you shouldn't underestimate the power of extrinsic rewards to bolster a group member's self-esteem and thus enhance his or her intrinsic motivation. Such rewards (including money) can also give a team the freedom to attempt experiments or to take risks that it otherwise wouldn't have had the means to do.

You probably won't have the leeway to create a formal compensation plan for your team. However, there are likely some areas where you have the power to tweak the company's existing system to your team's advantage. Ask yourself the following questions:

- Does my team need special incentives, distinct from the larger reward system of the organization as a whole? If so, what might those incentives look like?

- If I can't change the formal reward structure for my group, what informal awards can I design and distribute?

"Tips for motivating and rewarding creativity" provides additional recommendations.

Tips for motivating and rewarding creativity

- Ask a high-level executive to visit the team to express his/her appreciation of what the team is doing or to recognize the team's work.
- Give a reward for the craziest idea produced during a brainstorming session.
- Recognize a person who has worked outside his or her preferred style or function.
- Give a reward for collaboration.
- Give out small, visible symbols of recognition such as plaques, T-shirts, hats, toys, etc.

- Let team members choose which project they want to work on next.
- Celebrate a small success by taking the group out to dinner.
- Celebrate an interim deadline by taking off a half day to go to a movie together.
- Send out an e-mail, memo, group voice mail, or announcement describing (visually, if possible) how much work the group has done (e.g., printing out a list of all the orders received so far).
- Send out an e-mail, memo, group voice mail, or announcement sharing positive feedback from outsiders, customers, or upper management about progress to date.
- Organize a project fair in which everyone is encouraged to visit other team members (or other teams) to see what they are currently working on.
- Give team members some time off, or extra vacation days.

Creating the right physical environment

Just as the right psychological environment can foster creativity in your team, so can the right physical surroundings. When an environment is filled with many types of stimuli, it encourages people to make new connections and to think more broadly. It sends the message, "Think differently."

Truly creative environments are notable for the variety of art, toys, and reading material they contain. For example, a software company might include illustrated books on architectural design as well as technical reading in the employees' lounge. Another company might scatter wind-up toys or 3-D gadgets throughout the workspace. "Tips for enhancing the physical workspace" offers additional suggestions.

Tips for enhancing the physical workspace

- Put the kitchen and water cooler in a central location; you'll get people talking together more frequently about their ideas.
- Have a whiteboard or chalkboard that anyone can use in the kitchen and/or next to the water cooler to document ideas and thoughts as they occur.
- Have several comfortable, casual places for people to sit and chat.
- Have conference or meeting rooms easily accessible on short notice.
- Make the office space open, encouraging people to drop in on one another.
- Have a recognized and accepted signal that communicates when a person is working on a task that requires uninterrupted concentration (e.g., sign on door, movable partition across cube entrance).
- Put whiteboards, chalkboards, or flip charts in every meeting room.
- Have at least one electronic whiteboard from which you can print.
- Have paper, crayons, and colored pencils available during brain-storming sessions.
- Encourage people to draw or doodle ideas during meetings.
- Have videoconferencing technology available to link up with people who are not in your office.

- Have e-mail as well as electronic discussion databases or threaded discussion capabilities to allow ongoing discussion of key issues and problems.

A physical setting that encourages a playful attitude is especially important, because it helps people fully express their individuality and so enhances the quality of the group's creative output. Play serves a serious function: when employees are taking a play break, their work problems are incubating. The conscious mind takes a break from the problem at hand and is then able to return refreshed—perhaps with a new approach or a unique solution.

> *The workplace itself is alive with the unexpected; when employees interact with it, it yields provocations no one can possibly expect.*
> Alan Robinson and Sam Stern

Creative environments don't just provide casual and playful spaces—they also include areas where employees can be quiet and reflective. The goal is to open up the range of emotional responses people experience at work—quite a contrast from the traditional, "buttoned-down" approach to the work environment.

You may not be able to design your team's workspace from the ground up, but there are valuable—and relatively inexpensive—steps you can take to enhance your team's physical surroundings. As you consider your options, keep the following questions in mind:

- **How might you encourage casual conversations that lead to creative ideas?** Conversations and spontaneous meetings often occur around water coolers and in other public areas such as mailrooms or kitchens. Are these areas centrally located? Do you have comfortable, informal gathering places? One company designed staircases wide enough for people to stop and chat. Another placed beanbag chairs in conference rooms to create a more casual atmosphere.

- **What tools might you supply to encourage better communication?** Some companies place whiteboards and flip charts in informal meeting spaces—for example, the kitchen—rather than just in conference rooms. Making these tools available allows people to sketch out their ideas during a spontaneous discussion. Other companies distribute crayons and white paper on conference room tables to encourage people to doodle and diagram ideas—enabling a mode of thought that is quite different from verbal discussion.

- **What types of communication channels do team members prefer to use?** One person may find a lively discussion the most effective means of generating new ideas. Another may prefer the time and quiet afforded by e-mail communication. Still another may respond best to visual imagery. Including nontraditional communication channels and tools helps you capture the creative potential of *all* members of your group.

Step 4: Converge on the One Best Option

After your team has generated options for exploiting the opportunity it identified, it is time to converge on the one *best* option. Below are some suggestions for how to get to this point.

Moving from divergence to convergence

At various stages in the life of a project, the fruits of divergent thinking must be harvested and put to use. This process calls for the team to move from divergent thinking to convergent thinking. During the *convergent thinking* process, a team stops emphasizing what is novel and starts emphasizing what is useful. The work of convergence involves setting limits—narrowing the field of options using a given set of constraints.

Narrowing down the options

How do you determine the constraints appropriate for your team's convergent thinking? Think about your company's culture, mission, priorities, and resources, as well as the purpose of the creative project in which your team is involved. Evaluate each option your team generated according to these criteria. Rule out options that don't meet the criteria.

For example, suppose your team's creative effort centers on coming up with an idea for a new product. You can narrow down the list of options your team generated by asking some basic questions:

- What functions are "must-haves" for the product from our customers' point of view, and what functions are "nice-to-haves"?

- What criteria are determined by our company's values—for example, will the product have to work flawlessly every time?

- What are our cost constraints, and which of the options that we generated will fit within those constraints?

- What are the size or shape constraints for the new product?

- Within what time frame do we need to complete the project in order to capitalize on market demand?

- In what ways must the product be compatible with our company's existing products or services?

Answers to all these questions can help you and your team determine which option on your long list will *best* enable the team to transform its creative thinking into a valuable innovation.

Planning for innovation: The end product of creativity

As we mentioned earlier, innovation is an outcome of a team's creative process. It's the execution of the best option the team selects from its list of possible options. So once your team has narrowed down its list to the single most promising option, take some time to think about how this idea can be successfully implemented.

What Would YOU Do?

Playing with Ideas at PlayBig

EMILY OVERSEES THE NEW-PRODUCT DEVELOPMENT group at PlayBig, a company that makes video game software. Play-Big's senior management team has formulated a strategy hinging on bringing innovative products to market fast. For Emily and her team, the pressure is on to be original and cutting-edge with new offerings.

Emily assembles an intellectually diverse team including a few temporary members from other parts of the company. She introduces brainstorming techniques to help people come up with fresh ideas for new products—and deftly manages the resulting creative abrasion by reminding team members of the norms for interaction established by the group.

The team flourishes and eventually compiles a long list of exciting ideas and possibilities. Some are good and feasible; others seem downright risky. Emily senses that she needs to help the group move forward. But she's unsure of precisely how to do so. Should she start imposing constraints on the group's thinking process? What about analyzing each option the group has generated and assessing its market feasibility, costs, and so forth? Should she take a chance and get her group to commit to the riskiest of the options they're considering?

Her head is starting to spin . . .

What would YOU do? The mentor will suggest a solution in *What You COULD Do.*

For example, explore the following questions with your team:

- Whose help will we need to implement our idea?

- Why is each of these individual's help needed?

- What resources—such as money, office space, and equipment—will be essential for putting our idea into action?

- How will we get the resources we need?

- Who might resist our idea, and why? (For instance, would a manager of another product line view our new product as a threat?)

- How might we overcome resistance to the product?

- What short-term and long-term actions must be taken to implement our idea successfully?

- When should each action be carried out, and by whom?

- How will we measure successful implementation? (For instance, will sales of the new product reach a certain volume by a specified date?)

?What You COULD Do.

Remember Emily's uncertainty about how to move her product development team forward?

Here's what the mentor suggests:

Emily needs to help her group narrow the list of options they generated through divergent thinking—and eventually make a choice. It's time to shift from divergent to convergent thinking.

To help her team make this shift, Emily should impose an appropriate set of constraints. For example, does the team have a limited budget? Must they get their product to market before the end of the next fiscal year? How does the competition affect their choices?

A group determines its constraints by looking at a number of factors, such as the culture, mission, priorities, and high-level concept of the company and the project. A set of constraints helps a manager rule out options by identifying which potential solutions lie beyond the scope of the team's project. Depending on the constraints, Emily and her team may—or may not—decide on a risky solution.

Answers to these questions will help you and your team boost the odds of seeing that great, creative idea your team generated turned into a valuable new product, service, or business process for your company.

Tips and Tools

Tools for Fostering Creativity

CREATIVITY CHECKLIST

Use this checklist to assess the creativity dimension of your workplace.

Dimension	Rating		
	Adequate	A Strength	Needs Improvement
Your Leadership Style			
I can describe my own preferred style of thinking and working.			
I have talked with members of my group about their preferred modes of problem solving.			
I encourage intellectual conflict within my group.			
When group members disagree, I help them determine the source of their differences.			
When communicating with others, I take into consideration their preferred thinking style.			
Diversity of Styles			
I am aware of the creative value of diverse thinking styles and try to incorporate this diversity in teams.			
I actively seek out or hire people with diverse backgrounds and thinking styles.			
Our group recognizes the conflict that creative abrasion can cause but also recognizes its value.			
We have taken formal diagnostic tests to identify thinking or learning styles and discussed the results of these assessments.			
Your Work Group			
The majority never ignores the minority opinions in my work group.			

I have added someone to my work group specifically because he/she brings a fresh perspective.			
Our work environment supports those who think differently from the majority.			
The thinking styles, skills, and experiences of my work group's members are diverse and balanced.			
I actively look for group members whose thinking styles differ from my own.			
I help my group establish and agree upon a clear project goal at the start of each project.			
My group has agreed on formal behavior guidelines for how they should work together and treat one another			

The Psychological Environment

I support people taking intelligent risks and do not penalize them when they fail.			
There are opportunities for people to take on assignments that involve risk and stretch their potential.			
We openly discuss risk taking, assess the risk potential of projects, and make contingency plans or identify risk management strategies.			
Creative ideas receive rewards and/or recognition.			
As long as they show learning from the experience, group members are not penalized for experimentation and risk taking.			

The Physical Workspace

Our workspace includes stimulating objects such as journals, art, and other items that are not directly related to our business.			
I have made changes to our physical workspace to improve communication and stimulate creative interaction.			

I provide group members with a wide variety of traditional and nontraditional communication tools (e-mail, whiteboards, crayons and paper, etc.).			
Group members are encouraged to make their workspaces reflect their individuality.			
Our workspace includes *both* areas for boisterous interaction *and* areas for quiet reflection.			
Bringing in Outsiders or Alternative Perspectives			
Our group visits people outside the division or organization in order to find different perspectives and ideas.			
Our group has observed customers actually using our product or service *in their own environment.*			
Our group has observed our customers' customers using our product or service *in their own environment.*			
I have arranged for speakers from other industries to talk to or work with my group.			
Our group has observed people using competitors' products or services.			
Our group has benchmarked the functions and characteristics of our products, services, or internal processes against an industry other than our own.			
Promoting Group Convergence			
I encourage group members to bring up and discuss nonwork-related subjects when they interfere with work.			
When a project has been completed, I hold a debriefing to determine specifically what to do differently (or the same) the next time.			
When I hold a debriefing, I always make sure that all members can be present.			

When my group is stuck on a problem, I make sure they get "down time" or time off to step back, relax, and allow their subconscious minds to work.			
At the end of a project I provide a way for my group to celebrate and rejuvenate.			
Project schedules allow enough time for group brainstorming and discussion of ideas.			

Derived from *When Sparks Fly,* by Dorothy Leonard and Walter Swap (Harvard Business School Press, 1999).

SETTING A TARGET FOR CREATIVE CHANGE

Use this form to help you think through a creative change you would like to make, identifying what the benefits would be to you, your team, or your business.

Target

What is an area you want to target for creative input or change?

For example: new-product development, improved customer service, new marketing programs.

Within this area, what is the specific outcome or result you would like?

For example: five new ideas for next year's marketing programs for X product.

What kind of change are you looking for?

☐ adaptive (incremental change to existing structure)

☐ innovative (something novel or new)

What are the potential business benefits of this effort? What difference will it make?

For example: increased revenue, increased efficiency, increased customer satisfaction, etc.

What are the personal or team benefits of this effort?

Team

What is the current creative makeup of the team members who will work on this creative challenge?

Member	Role/How (s)he can contribute	Preferred thinking style*(1, 2, 3, or 4)

* 1 *Rational:* logical, analytical, fact-based 2 *Experimental:* intuitive, risk-taking, integrative
3 *Organized:* planner, detail-oriented 4 *Feeling:* interpersonal, emotional, feelings-based

Do you have the right mix of styles to encourage creativity? And the expertise required?
☐ Yes ☐ No. Additional styles needed: ☐ No. Additional expertise needed:
Do you have the in-house resources to meet these needs? If not, how can you bring in outsiders or others to fill in the gaps? *For example, hire a consultant with technical expertise.*
Where is the team currently stuck? What behaviors tell you this?
What measures can help minimize or overcome these obstacles?
Techniques *Select creative techniques you'll use.*
Brainstorming techniques (producing lots of original ideas while suspending judgment):

☐ *Visioning* (for example, imagining, in detail, an ideal solution)

☐ *Experimenting* (such as combining elements in novel ways and then testing combinations)

☐ *Modifying* (generating new ideas by expanding on or adapting what already exists)

☐ *Exploratory* (such as guided imagery, use of analogies, metaphors)

Creative problem-solving techniques:
Other:

Time Frame

Kick-off date:	Desired completion date:
Reasons for target time:	

Planned sequence of events:

Activity	Date	Person Responsible

Communication Plan	
What information needs to be communicated, to whom, and by when?	
Who has input into the process? Who are the stakeholders? Who has veto power?	
What communication vehicles or tools will you use?	
Who needs to be informed of progress?	When?
Who needs to be informed of results?	When?
Who on the creative team is taking responsibility for communicating the process and results? For gaining alignment and agreement?	

PSYCHOLOGICAL ENVIRONMENT FOR CREATIVITY ASSESSMENT

Use this assessment to evaluate how your current reward structure, group norms and attitudes, and management style support creativity.

Question	Rating		
	Adequate	A Strength	Needs Improvement
1. Are group guidelines already in place? Are they articulated and disseminated?			
2. Do you, as the manager, encourage risk taking?			
3. Are people allowed to take intelligent risks, and fail, without being penalized?			
4. When someone fails, do you help that person and the group find the learning in the failure?			
5. Do you distinguish between intelligent failures (something risky, but promising) and mistakes (something clearly avoidable)?			
6. Do your current rewards motivate group members to be creative?			
7. Do you currently have rewards for creative ideas/suggestions?			
8. Does your current reward system offer both extrinsic (for example, money) and intrinsic (for example, providing a sense of accomplishment) rewards?			
9. Do you recognize group members who successfully work outside their preferred thinking style or area of expertise?			
10. Do you support intellectual conflict within your group?			
11. Do you encourage people to point out unacknowledged and taboo subjects that are holding the group back?			
12. Do you reward collaboration?			

13. Do individuals have freedom to choose their projects or to determine how they reach their agreed-upon goals?			
14. Are you, as a manager, alert to individuals who may be burning out?			
15. Do you celebrate small successes?			
16. Do you encourage the group to stop and review how much progress it has made?			

Ideas for Improvement

Based on your answers, what refinements would you make to your group's norms? To your reward structure? To your own management style?

Derived from *When Sparks Fly,* by Dorothy Leonard and Walter Swap (Harvard Business School Press, 1999).

ENHANCING THE CREATIVITY OF THE PHYSICAL WORKSPACE

Use this worksheet to conduct an inventory of your physical workspace and generate ideas for improvements that take into account the level of alteration that is possible.

Dimension	Current Condition	Ideas for Improvement
Accessible, casual meeting space		
Physical stimuli (for example, books, videos, art on walls, journals)		
Space for quiet reflection		
Variety of communication tools (for example, whiteboards, bulletin boards, e-mail)		
Employee-only space		
Customer contact space		
Space for individual expression		

Game or relaxation area		

Derived from *When Sparks Fly,* by Dorothy Leonard and Walter Swap (Harvard Business School Press, 1999).

FORM FOR LISTING ATTRIBUTES

Use this form to generate ideas about how you could improve upon any one or more attributes or qualities to enhance a product, process, or procedure. List the attributes in one column, ideas for improvement in the other. This task can be done as a solo activity, but it may be more effective with a group.

Target: *Product, process, or service that you are seeking to improve*

Attributes	Ideas for Improvement
Example: A bike has a frame	Make the frame lighter

Test Yourself

This section offers ten multiple-choice questions to help you identify your baseline knowledge of marketing. Answers to the questions are given at the end of the test.

1. The process of evaluating ideas to determine which are worth pursuing is called

   a. Divergent thinking.

   b. Convergent thinking.

   c. Innovation.

2. Which of the following statements are true? A. Creativity is a talent that you either have or don't have; B. The creative process is basically a solitary pursuit; C. The smarter you are, the more creative you are; D. Age is not a clear predictor of creativity.

   a. A and B.

   b. All of the above.

   c. D.

3. Most innovative ideas are the result of a conscious, purposeful search, not sudden illumination. True or false?

   a. True.

   b. False.

4. Creative groups often need to balance contradictory behaviors or characteristics to generate fresh ideas. Which of the following pairs of contradictory behaviors and characteristics does a group *not* need to balance in order to strengthen its creativity?

   a. Beginner's mind and experienced perspective.

   b. Freedom and discipline.

   c. Improvisation and planning.

   d. Focus on process and focus on results.

   e. Play and professionalism.

5. Creative abrasion occurs when

   a. Individuals' thinking styles clash, forcing them to examine new ways of looking at an issue.

   b. Individuals' thinking styles are compatible, allowing the group to develop new ideas quickly.

   c. Individuals in the group dislike one another, preventing them from collaborating effectively.

6. Intellectual diversity and different thinking styles can generate conflict in a group. This substantive conflict is the same as personal conflict. True or false?

   a. True.

   b. False.

7. Rewards of various kinds can improve a group's creativity. Pay and bonuses are examples of rewards that tap into an individual's

a. Extrinsic motivation.

b. Intrinsic motivation.

8. You're conducting a brainstorming session and team members are evaluating options and ideas as they generate them. Is this the best way to proceed?

a. Yes.

b. No.

9. Which of the following techniques or strategies is *not* useful for brainstorming?

a. Using guided imagery to describe an ideal scenario.

b. Keeping constraints such as time and money in mind while envisioning possible ideal solutions.

c. Looking at ways to adapt the status quo, rather than invent from the beginning.

d. Systematically combining elements of a project or product in different ways and then testing these new combinations.

10. A "moose on the table" is an expression used to describe an issue that a group is ignoring or avoiding that could become a problem and impede progress. Which of the following would you *not* do to deal effectively with a "moose"?

a. Stop what you are doing to acknowledge the issue.

b. If the issue involves someone's behavior, discuss it one-on-one outside the group.

c. Encourage the person who identified the moose to be specific and to use examples.

d. Discuss *what* is impeding progress, not *who*.

Answers to test questions

1, b. Convergent thinking is often an evaluative process whereby different options are reviewed to determine which are worth pursuing.

2, c. The only true statement in the list is that "age is not a clear predictor of creativity." The other three statements represent common misconceptions about creativity.

3, a. Most innovative ideas are not so much the product of sudden insights as they are the result of a conscious process that often goes through multiple stages.

4, d. While a group often needs to balance concern for process (how the group is working together) with concern for results, this balancing is not essential to a group's creative functioning.

5, a. The creative abrasion created by individuals' different thinking styles can greatly enhance a group's creative potential if it is well managed.

6, b Substantive conflict and personal conflict are actually different. Substantive conflict occurs when members grapple with issues or tasks at hand—for example, when two members of the group challenge each other's assumptions. In contrast, personal conflict has no relation to the tasks at hand.

7, a. Pay and bonuses are extrinsic motivators: They appeal to a person's desire to attain a goal that is distinct from the work itself. But to encourage your group's creativity, you should augment extrinsic motivators with intrinsic motivators, such as challenging assignments. Intrinsic motivators appeal to a person's desire for self-actualization or challenge, deep interest and involvement in the work, or curiosity or sense of enjoyment.

8, b. Evaluating options or ideas as they are generated can stifle creativity and slow down the group's brainstorming process.

9, b. Keeping constraints such as time and money in mind while trying to envision an ideal solution is not a useful brainstorming technique. Rather, individuals should try to break free of the ingrained practicality that inhibits innovative thought.

10, b. Discussing a behavior-related issue *within* the group is an advisable strategy for dealing with a "moose on the table." The issue needs to be surfaced, discussed, and resolved in terms of the impact of the behavior on the group. During this discussion it is important to keep things impersonal. The point is not to assign blame—discuss *what* is impeding progress, not *who*.

To Learn More

Articles

Amabile, Teresa M. "Managing for Creativity." Harvard Business School Case Note. Boston: Harvard Business School Publishing, 1996.

After discussing environmental stimuli and obstacles to creativity, this article addresses the delicate balance involved in managing for creativity. It also describes a questionnaire instrument for assessing an organization's climate for creativity.

Drucker, Peter F. "The Discipline of Innovation." *Harvard Business Review* OnPoint Enhanced Edition. Boston: Harvard Business School Publishing, 2000.

In this HBR Classic article, Peter Drucker, professor emeritus at Claremont Graduate University, argues that success is more likely to result from the systematic pursuit of opportunities than from a flash of genius. For managers seeking innovation, engaging in disciplined work is more important than having an entrepreneurial personality. Drucker explains that internal opportunities for innovation can be found in unexpected occurrences, incongruities of various kinds, process needs, or changes in an industry or market; externally, such opportunities arise from demographic changes, changes in perception, or new knowledge. Drucker emphasizes that in seeking opportunities, innovators need to look for simple, focused solutions to real problems.

Florida, Richard. "America's Looming Creativity Crisis." *Harvard Business Review,* October 2004.

In this article the author argues that the strength of the U.S. economy turns on one factor—the country's openness to new ideas—which has allowed it to attract the brightest minds from around the world and harness their creative energies. However, he suggests, the United States is on the verge of losing that competitive edge. To defend the U.S. economy, the business community must take the lead in ensuring that global talent can move efficiently across borders, that education and research are funded at radically higher levels, and that we tap into the creative potential of more and more workers.

Florida, Richard, and Jim Goodnight. "Managing for Creativity." *Harvard Business Review* OnPoint Enhanced Edition. Boston: Harvard Business School Publishing, February 2007.

How do you accommodate the complex and chaotic nature of the creative process while increasing efficiency, improving quality, and raising productivity? Most businesses haven't figured this out. A notable exception is SAS Institute, the world's largest privately held software company. SAS has learned how to harness the creative energies of all its stakeholders— including its customers, software developers, managers, and support staff. Its framework for managing creativity rests on three guiding principles. First, help employees do their best work by keeping them intellectually engaged and by removing distractions. Second, make managers responsible for sparking creativity and eliminate arbitrary distinctions between "suits" and "creatives." And third, engage customers as creative partners so that you can deliver superior products.

Hargadon, Andrew, and Robert I. Sutton. "Building an Innovation Factory." *Harvard Business Review* OnPoint Enhanced Edition. Boston: Harvard Business School Publishing, 2001.

New ideas are the precious currency of the new economy, but generating them doesn't have to be a mysterious process. The image of the lone genius inventing from scratch is a romantic fiction. Businesses that constantly innovate have systematized the production and testing of new ideas, and the system can be replicated by practically any organization. The best innovators use old ideas as the raw materials for new ideas, a strategy the authors call knowledge brokering. The system for sustaining innovation is the knowledge-brokering cycle, and the authors discuss its four stages: (1) Capture good ideas from a wide variety of sources. (2) Keep those ideas alive by playing with them, discussing them, and using them. (3) Imagine new uses for old ideas—some knowledge brokers encourage cross-pollination by creating physical layouts that allow, or even force, people to interact with one another. (4) Turn promising concepts into real services, products, processes, or business models. Companies can use all or part of the cycle. Large companies in particular desperately need to move ideas from one place to another. Some will want to build full-fledged consulting groups dedicated to internal knowledge brokering. Others can hire people who have faced problems similar to the companies' current problems. The most important lesson is that business leaders must change how they think about innovation, and they must change how their company cultures reflect that thinking.

Harvard Business School Publishing. "Debriefing Luc de Brabandere: Boost Your Company's Creativity." *Harvard Management Update,* April 2006.

Today, popular tastes mutate continually, and technologies advance at a blistering pace. Businesses must continually innovate to keep up. But leaders who can't detect and respond to rumblings of change—that is, who can't be creative—stand little chance of generating these innovations. The key to creativity, according to Luc de Brabandere, a partner in the Boston Consulting Group, is learning to articulate and change the stereotypes that limit us. In this debriefing, he outlines four rules managers can follow to circumvent these blocks and hone creative powers.

Books

Davis, Howard, and Richard Scase. *Managing Creativity: The Dynamics of Work and Organization.* Buckingham, England: Open University Press, 2001.

The creative industries are a growing economic as well as cultural force. This book investigates their organizational dynamics and shows how companies structure their work processes to incorporate creative employees' needs for autonomy while at the same time controlling and coordinating their output.

Leonard, Dorothy, and Walter Swap. *When Sparks Fly: Igniting Creativity in Groups*. Boston: Harvard Business School Press, 1999.

Where do the best creative ideas come from? Most managers assume that it's the readily identifiable "creative types" that offer the quickest route to out-of-the-box, breakthrough thinking, and that if you don't have an eccentric genius on your team, your group is doomed to mediocrity. Yet, say Leonard and Swap, most innovations today spring from well-led group interactions. In *When Sparks Fly,* the authors reveal that any group—if designed and managed effectively—can produce more innovative services, products, and processes. Unlike most books on creativity, *When Sparks Fly* focuses on the process as it applies to groups of people who may not fit the stereotype of right-brained "creatives." Leonard and Swap offer managers strategies for generating the group dynamics that lie at the heart of innovative thinking, including specific techniques for rechanneling the tensions of conflicting points of view into new ideas and alternative options. *When Sparks Fly* explores how all aspects of the work environment—from leadership style to the use of space, sound, even smell—can enhance innovation.

Miller, William C. *Flash of Brilliance*. Reading, MA: Perseus Books, 1999.

Miller emphasizes the ways in which an individual's values and spirituality enrich and inform his or her creativity. But the book also includes concrete suggestions for overcoming obstacles to creativity and provides an extended treatment of four basic approaches to brainstorming.

eLearning programs

Harvard Business School Publishing. Case in Point. Boston: Harvard Business School Publishing, 2004.

Case in Point is a flexible set of online cases designed to help prepare middle- and senior-level managers for a variety of leadership challenges. These short, reality-based scenarios provide sophisticated content to create a focused insight into the realities of the life of a leader. Your managers will delve into Aligning Strategy, Removing Implementation Barriers, Overseeing Change, Anticipating Risk, Ethical Decisions, Building a Business Case, Cultivating Customer Loyalty, Emotional Intelligence, Developing a Global Perspective, Fostering Innovation, Defining Problems, Selecting Solutions, Managing Difficult Interactions, The Coach's Role, Delegating for Growth, Managing Creativity, Influencing Others, Managing Performance, Providing Feedback, and Retaining Talent.

Sources for Fostering Creativity

The following sources aided in development of this book:

Amabile, Teresa M. "Creativity and Innovation in Organizations." Harvard Business School Case Note # N9-396-239, January 5, 1996.

Barrett, Derm. *The Paradox Process*. New York: AMACOM, 1997.

Cannon, Mark, and Amy Edmondson. "Confronting Failure: Antecedents and Consequences of Shared Learning-Oriented Beliefs in Organizational Work Groups." 1999 (under review by an academic journal).

Csikszentmihalyi, Mihaly. *Creativity: Flow and the Psychology of Discovery and Invention*. New York: HarperCollins, 1996.

Drucker, Peter. "The Discipline of Innovation." *Harvard Business Review,* November–December 1998.

Isaksen, Scott G., K. Brian Dorval, and Donald J. Treffinger. *Creative Approaches to Problem Solving*. Dubuque, IA: Kendall/Hunt Publishing Company, 1994.

Isaksen, Scott G., K. Brian Dorval, and Donald J. Treffinger. *Toolbox for Creative Problem Solving.* Williamsville, NY: Creative Problem Solving Group–Buffalo, 1998.

Leonard, Dorothy. *Managing Groups for Creativity and Innovation.* Boston: Harvard Business School Press, 1998.

Leonard, Dorothy, and Walter Swap. *When Sparks Fly: Igniting Creativity in Groups.* Boston: Harvard Business School Press, 1999.

Michalko, Michael. *Cracking Creativity: The Secrets of Creative Genius.* Berkeley, CA: Ten Speed Press, 1998.

Miller, William C. *Flash of Brilliance.* Reading, MA: Perseus Books, 1999.

Robinson, Alan G., and Sam Stern. *Corporate Creativity.* San Francisco: Berrett-Koehler, 1997.

Saunders, Rebecca M. "Better Brainstorming." *Harvard Management Communication Letter,* November 1999.

Zelinski, Ernie J. *The Joy of Thinking Big.* Berkeley, CA: Ten Speed Press, 1998.

Notes

Notes

Notes

How to Order

Harvard Business School Press publications are available world-wide from your local bookseller or online retailer.

You can also call:
1-800-668-6780

Our product consultants are available to help you 8:00 a.m.–6:00 p.m., Monday–Friday, Eastern Time. Outside the U.S. and Canada, call: 617-783-7450.

Please call about special discounts for quantities greater than ten.

You can order online at:
www.HBSPress.org